Dear Parents and Educators,

Welcome to Penguin Young Readers! As parents and educators, you know that each child develops at his or her own pace—in terms of speech, critical thinking, and, of course, reading. Penguin Young Readers recognizes this fact. As a result, each Penguin Young Readers book is assigned a traditional easy-to-read level (1–4) as well as a Guided Reading Level (A–P). Both of these systems will help you choose the right book for your child. Please refer to the back of each book for specific leveling information. Penguin Young Readers features esteemed authors and illustrators, stories about favorite characters, fascinating nonfiction, and more!

Pig-Piggy-Pigs

LEVEL **2**

GUIDED READING LEVEL **I**

This book is perfect for a **Progressing Reader** who:
• can figure out unknown words by using picture and context clues;
• can recognize beginning, middle, and ending sounds;
• can make and confirm predictions about what will happen in the text; and
• can distinguish between fiction and nonfiction.

Here are some **activities** you can do during and after reading this book:
• Nonfiction: Nonfiction books deal with facts and events that are real. Talk about the elements of nonfiction. Discuss some of the facts you learned about pigs. Then answer the following questions: Why do pigs roll in mud? What are baby pigs called? Which body part do pigs use to find food? What do pigs eat?
• Homophones: Homophones are words that sound alike but have different meanings. In this book, the words *here* and *hear* are homophones. Think of homophones for these other words from the book: *roll*, *tail*, and *weigh*.

Remember, sharing the love of reading with a child is the best gift you can give!

—Bonnie Bader, EdM
  Penguin Young Readers program

*Penguin Young Readers are leveled by independent reviewers applying the standards developed by Irene Fountas and Gay Su Pinnell in *Matching Books to Readers: Using Leveled Books in Guided Reading*, Heinemann, 1999.

For Lauren, who wants a pig!—BB

PENGUIN YOUNG READERS
An Imprint of Penguin Random House LLC

Photo credits: cover: © Brittany Williford; flap: © Thinkstock/atosan; page 3: © Thinkstock/Tsekhmister; page 4: © Thinkstock/Eric Isselée; page 5: © Thinkstock/chengyuzheng; pages 6–7: © Getty Images/Bill Ling; page 8: (small pig) © Thinkstock/Tsekhmister, (big pig) © Thinkstock/Eric Isselée, (black piglet) © Thinkstock/Aumsama; page 9: (black pig) © Thinkstock/adogslifephoto, (laying pig) © Thinkstock/a4ndreas; page 10: © Getty Images/E.A. Janes; page 11: © Thinkstock/wanderluster; page 12: © Getty Images/Mike Dabell; page 13: © Getty Images/Simon Clay; pages 14–15: © Francine Fleischer/Corbis; page 16: © Thinkstock/atosan; page 17: © Thinkstock/a4ndreas; page 18: © Thinkstock/FRANCO DI MEO; page 19: © Thinkstock/TERRY SWARTZ; page 21: © Thinkstock/Jevtic; page 22: (pig walker) © Getty Images/MoMo Productions, (pig sniffing) © Thinkstock/galyna66, (litter box) © Thinkstock/Dmytro_Skorobogatov; page 23: (pig bed) © Thinkstock/kuban_girl, (blanket) © Thinkstock/belchonock, (pig blanket) © Thinkstock/adogslifephoto; pages 24–25: © Thinkstock/Fuse; pages 26–27: (small pig) © Thinkstock/Tsekhmister, (carrots) © Thinkstock/Diana Taliun, (grapes) © Thinkstock/philg24, (raisins) © Thinkstock/Ingram Publishing, (water bowl) © Thinkstock/PahaM; page 28: © Thinkstock/Tsekhmister; page 29: © Thinkstock/afhunta; page 30: © Thinkstock/Zelenenka; page 31: © Getty Images/Matthias Clamer; page 32: © Getty Images/PeopleImages.com.

Text copyright © 2015 by Bonnie Bader. All rights reserved. Published by Penguin Young Readers, an imprint of Penguin Random House LLC, 345 Hudson Street, New York, New York 10014. Manufactured in China.

Library of Congress Cataloging-in-Publication Data is available.

ISBN 978-0-448-48221-7 (pbk)   10 9 8 7 6 5 4
ISBN 978-0-448-48222-4 (hc)   10 9 8 7 6 5 4 3 2 1

Pig-Piggy-Pigs

by Bonnie Bader

Penguin Young Readers
An Imprint of Penguin Random House

Pig.

Piggy.

Pigs.

Some pigs are big.

Some pigs are small.

But they all have cute noses

and curly tails.

Some people think pigs are dirty
animals.

But they are not.

Pigs are clean.

They only roll in mud
when they are hot.

Baby pigs are called piglets.

Piglets are very tiny

when they are born.

They weigh about

two and a half pounds.

Piglets drink their mother's milk
for three to five weeks.
Then they are old enough
to live on their own.

Pigs can't see very well.

But they can smell very well.

Pigs use their noses, or snouts,

to look for food.

Some pigs make good pets.
But you have to be sure you really
want one.

Find out if it is okay to have a pig

in your town.

Make sure it is okay with

your family.

Some people get big pigs as pets.

This is a potbellied pig.

She is 150 pounds.

She can grow to be 250 pounds!

Some people get small pigs

as pets.

This is a teacup pig.

She is only 12 pounds now.

But she can grow to be

60 pounds.

Or more!

You have to take good care

of your pig.

Your pig will need to visit

the doctor.

The doctor will look at your pig

to make sure it is healthy.

Your pig will get some shots.

Just like you do when you go

to the doctor.

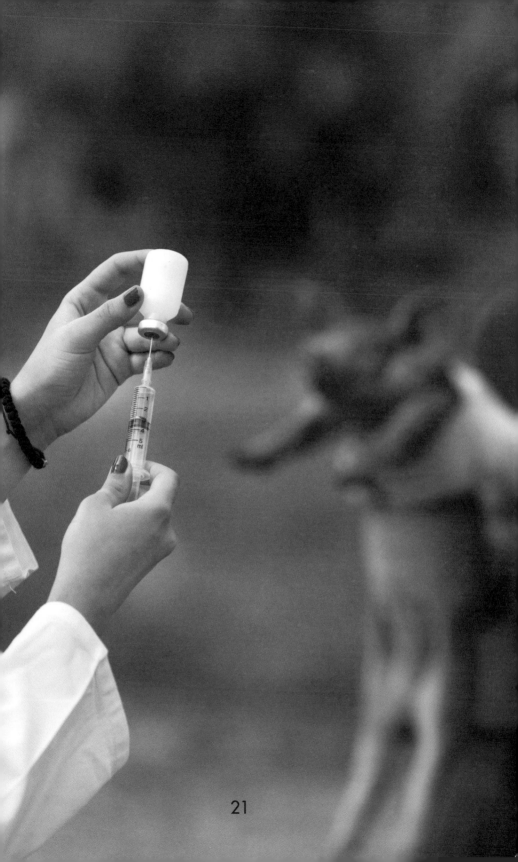

You can teach your pig

to walk on a leash.

You can teach your pig

to use a litter box.

Your pig can sleep

inside your house.

Make a bed for your pig.

And give your pig a blanket.

Pigs are very smart.

They are even smarter

than dogs.

You can teach your pig tricks.

Sit. Shake. Roll over. Good job!

Your pig needs to eat
the right food.
Buy pig food at
a pet store.

Your pig can also eat grapes,

raisins, and carrots.

And always have clean water

for your pig to drink.

Pigs like to go outside to play.

Make sure your outdoor space

is safe.

You should have a fence

so your pig will not run away.

Pigs like to dig.

Give your pig a space

in your backyard

where she can dig.

Your pig might not stay small.

She could grow big.

But you will always love your pig.

And she will always love you.